MW01491339

"In this well-written short book, Michelle Jarvie has captured and written about the stinging truth of sudden traumatic loss in a way that every young widow will relate to. Her difficult and challenging journey through grief to renewed life is raw, hopeful and inspiring."
> – Pamela D. Blair, Ph.D., Co-author, *I Wasn't Ready to Say Goodbye*

"There are too few books about young widows or widowers. There are fewer books about grief and bereavement as honest, raw, and revealing as Jarvie's. While it is one person's account of her immediate there and then feelings and thoughts following by her later reflections, *Then & Now* is also a book that captures the arc of loss, grief, healing, and hope that many experience. Just as losses themselves should be handled with care, the reader of this volume should be prepared for the deep valleys of grief and a life of living with loss...and hope."
> – Ted Bowman, Grief and Family Educator

"Bold. Strong. Beautiful. Ms. Jarvie takes on her own pain head on. She tells her truth with no apologies and brings you through to her 'next'- changed and transformed."
> – Molly DePrekel, M.A., L.P., Clinical Director at Cairns Psychological Services

"After thirty years as a victim advocate helping victims of traffic crashes, I feel this book will be beneficial to individuals who have been impacted by a devastating crash resulting in the death or injury of a loved one. It is an honest and insightful account of one woman's experiences after the tragic death of her young husband. It is a blessing she found her way and is able to help others by telling her story."

– Sharon Gehrman-Driscoll, Director/Victim Advocate at Minnesotans for Safe Driving

THEN & Now

Michelle D. Jarvie

THEN & *Now*

CHANGED PERSPECTIVES
of
A YOUNG WIDOW

Michelle D. Jarvie

MOVIS LAKE PRESS
Minneapolis, MN.

www.michellejarvie.com

Cover design by Islam Farid

Printed in the United States of America

First edition, 2015.

ISBN-13: 978-1503223639
ISBN-10:1503223639

Published by Movis Lake Press
Minneapolis, MN

For Jessica

I wish the whole world could experience having a friend like you. Thank you for helping me walk down another street.

Kes: "Everything seems so different now … How can I go back to my normal life?"

Tuvok: "You cannot. This experience will force you to adapt. You are no longer the same person, and the course of your life will change as a result. Where that new course leads is up to you."

- From "Warlord," *Star Trek: Voyager*

Table of Contents

Acknowledgements

To all the people who told me this book will make a difference and needs to be published, especially Jessica Johnson, Jeff Mosner, Olga Mosner, Beth Horsch, Nick Kramer, Victoria Wilson, and Susan Rode. The conversations we've held when I was excited, wanted to quit, or needed reassurance will never be forgotten.

Special thanks to those who listen, inspire, and value sharing raw emotions, especially Peggy McCalla, John Strommen, Kari Schuch, Ben Gallagher, Erin Longenecker, Wendy Wolfe, Charles Mosner, Lisa Hansen, Sandy Sorenson, Brent Warr, Molly Senser, Mikaela Schultz, Shannon McKeeth and Marv Davis.

To my new friend and editor, Carrie Hitchcock, who pushed me to look even deeper in my word choices and the "true" nature of sadness and acceptance.

Finally, thank you to my husband, Sean. Your patience, love, and empathy continue to make me fall deeper in love with you every day. I could not have published this book without your support.

Introduction

When my husband died, I read over a dozen books on grief and widowhood in the first two months. My liberal estimate of those books that helped me in the hours I craved death is three (see Appendix B). One of my main problems was feeling dramatically different from the bereaved person sharing their story: Most were middle-aged mothers or seniors who experienced at least a decade of marriage to their husbands. I was in the honeymoon stage after only 13 months, weeks away from buying my first house with my husband where we dreamed of raising four children. When J died, all of our dreams died with him. And I had the rest of my life – probably around 60 years – to go it alone.

Since our time together was so short and idyllic, I was further discouraged from relating to authors who talked about moving on and opening one's heart again. I was not interested in that at all. I wondered in judgment: Did they not love their husbands as much as I loved mine? It was difficult not to ask this every time a well-intentioned person told me that I was young and pretty and would find someone else. A few select individuals felt my anger while I relayed my resentment of their insinuation that J could be replaced or that my young age made anything easier.

A second problem between me and these other widows was how their home life pulled them out of dark moments. Most cited their children: If the widow was older, their teenage or adult children were a great support to help with the chores, finances, etc.; if younger, taking care of little children occupied their time and served as a way to honor their husbands. Pretending to converse with the authors, I asked, "So what am I supposed to do as a childless widow when I come home to my empty house?" If there was an answer to that question, I never read it.

Friends and family recommended that I get out of the house and go talk with people face-to-face, like counselors or other widows, in a group setting. However, I encountered similar problems, because there were no other young widows under the age of 45, and even then 95% of the women I met knew their husbands were going to die from an illness. They spent months or years in preparation, on a roller coaster of hope and despair. I had a state trooper show up and tell me J died instantly because someone wasn't paying attention on the freeway, rear-ended him on his stopped motorcycle, and dragged him 300 feet to his death. I can't and won't say that his sudden death is worse than watching someone deteriorate for years due to cancer, for example, but I will say that it is very different. And I think that is okay to acknowledge. The counselors, of course, never met a widow in her twenties, and their advice could be summarized in one statement: Trauma takes time. So the unsurprising conclusion was that I felt no one could understand me, let alone help me.

I am writing this book in the hope that I can

provide simple yet powerful reflections that don't take three hours to read *and* reach out to the uncommon widow. I enjoy reading 300-page chapter books when they are mysteries and I have hours to devote attention, but not when I'm drowning in misery, pity, daunting realities, and people who have no experience with my particular grief. Therefore, it's important to me to make the following promises: (1) You can finish this book in about an hour, and (2) I will provide tangible recommendations for moving forward and finding ways to carry the pain and not be destroyed by it.

This book is broken up into nine short chapters excluding the introduction you're reading as well as an epilogue and two appendices. What's significant about each section relates to the title of the book: Then & Now. The first half of each section describes the nauseating-weakening-seething feelings about the topics that crippled me in my first year. It is meant to validate and describe the sheer hell that is endured. The second half presents changed perspectives through time on those feelings that allow me to now cope and live. Thus, they are reflections on my feelings at the beginning ("Then") and how I process things today, six years later ("Now"). I believe self-reflection is the most imperative quality in human beings, and we do ourselves – and the world – a disservice by ignoring it. Some people do it through writing, some through music, some through art, and some through nature. I think I have used all of these methods, and I know they are invaluable to letting myself feel and finding the answers within.

Michelle Jarvie

Chapter 1: Well-Intentioned People

THEN

How dare you. Our society is so afraid of people crying, not being okay, remembering the hard times, that they try to band-aid with these classic lines:

"God has a plan." God means for a young, happily married man, who can't wait to be a dad, to get rear-ended and dragged under a car for 300 feet until he dies? Did God make the other driver get on the same highway as J and purposefully distract her so that she wouldn't see him? What kind of God is watching over us when He lets murderers and rapists find loopholes in the system, and at the same time lets people like J – who didn't have an angry

1

bone in his body – die in such a senseless way?

"He never gives us more than we can handle." I get that you want me to believe I'll be okay (which I don't), but what I hear is: J's death went according to God's design and my reaction is some sort of test. What kind of cruel being would ever put someone through this much pain on purpose? And who said I even believe in God? Don't assume that every mourner turns to faith or that platitudes are around because they're helpful.

"I know how you feel." No, you don't. So your grandma or sister or uncle died, and you know how it feels to lose your life partner and dreams? You weren't going to have children or grow old with those people. I bet you even had someone to go home to and share your grief. Moreover, what do you know about meeting the State Patrol at your door, seeing a reconstruction of the crash, and reading the 16-page autopsy report that notes blood-filled lungs and tire marks on his abdomen? That other driver rear-ended him with a revoked license and no insurance, but because she wasn't on drugs or alcohol, nobody in the legal system cares. It's not even manslaughter – reckless driving is a misdemeanor. When you tailgate other vehicles like she did, or use your phone while driving, you certainly don't understand.

"Good things come out of tragedies." And you think that right now is the time to tell me that there is good within my husband's death? Are you trying to prevent me from being angry and sad by guilting me into some higher philosophy of life? This seems like a statement that people want to believe is true, so that they can rationalize why bad things happen.

"You're young, you'll find someone else!" I want to die because I can't stand the thought of living without the man I committed the rest of my life to, and you think it's appropriate to tell me how I'll be in love again and have another family? How dare you insinuate that J is replaceable and that my age should lessen my grief.

How dare you.

NOW

The truth is that most people are unintentionally untrustworthy. In other words, they are ignorant of emotional truths. The result of these complicated phrases is that I'm careful whom I talk to about J and my pain. No one honors him and the beautiful life we led by hearing me share the most precious story in my heart and then telling me that with time, I'll let him go and start over. I've learned that most people are uncomfortable with my pain not only because it stirs feelings of their own mortality and/or that of their loved ones, but also because our culture is not one that sits well with suffering. Very few of my friends and family could listen to me talk and restrain themselves from trying to fix the situation; consequently, like many widows, my address book completely changed. And when I say changed, I mean people disappeared.

Six years later, I know that most people just have no idea what to say to me and so they do what they know: repeat clichés. Actually, I've come to a point where I'm more aggravated if someone can't find the strength to even acknowledge the fact that my husband was killed. Everyone deserves at least this much: "I'm so sorry for your loss. I can't imagine how hard it is to lose your partner."

Years of tears and reflection finally taught me that I need to be assertive when people resort to clichés and can't say the simple line above. Thus, the following are the lines I now have in my pocket for well-intentioned people who say ignorant things:

(1) "I know that you're trying to make me feel better, and I appreciate that you care. But I'm not in a place where I can listen to what you're saying and not feel worse. What I need is for you to listen and be okay with wherever I'm at right now."

(2) "Please stop talking. I appreciate that you want to help,

but there is nothing you can do or say that will get me to a better place. I can only get there on my own."

(3) "I know you believe what you're saying, but it's not helpful to me right now."

Regarding the God comments, I was fortunate to talk with a Harvard-educated pastor about my questions and the weight of people's expectations that I turn to God. He told me there is a difference between a plan and a script. God has large-scale plans for humanity, but He cannot have a script because He gave everyone the gift of free will. This pastor also argued there are many forces at work that we can't begin to understand, even through broad terms like chaos theory. God and life are mysteries.

Further, it is specifically through moments of pain that we appreciate how wondrous something can be. We may yearn for the blissful ignorance of youth – before we were touched by despairing realities of adulthood – but pure joy comes from acceptance that hardships will always be with us. For when we acknowledge this truth and reflect on our barren times, we cherish and live in the present like never before.

Six years later, that finally makes sense. Yet, I still struggle holding onto that truth all of the time. For example, there are moments when my Post-Traumatic Stress Disorder (PTSD) is triggered and I can't stop picturing J die. I rock myself back and forth like a child and try to remember my therapists' suggestions. In those moments, the crippling pain from his death makes me wish I'd never met him. But I know this is not true every time I look at the scrapbook I made of our life together. It holds beautiful poems he left on my pillow – sometimes through post-it notes – that ask "How does she like being married on day 86?" and "What is it about you that causes me to love you so much?" The pages detail our Minnesota adventures with peacocks and icicles (not at the same time), getting lost on the way home from our wedding, our reunion after I took a job in Maryland, and the house we were weeks away from buying. It captures the names of the children we hoped to bring into this world, songs we sang on our anniversary, and photoshopped pictures of who really hogs the bed. It took many years for me to see happiness in this scrapbook, as for a long time my identity was so tied to the memories that I could only feel what I'd lost.

Just as Garth Brooks sang in his famous song, "The Dance," I was the king. I loved my life so much, especially coming home. J would run down the stairs with arms open and say: "How's my hot little Ukrainian wife?" Then we'd make dinner together, take an hour to eat because we loved talking to one another, and relax with our books (or *Star Trek*) by a fire. I remember losing myself in thought, wondering how life could feel so easy, so perfect. Even though I could've missed the terrible pain of his death had I never met him, I would've missed our dance. As I now live in acceptance of how life really works, I can experience true joy when I look at the scrapbook and when I move forward, engaging in my present life knowing how I want to live.

Chapter 2: Depression

THEN

I used to love food. I knew the minute to pull out chicken from the oven for ultimate tenderness. Now, I've lost 30 pounds in one month because food tastes like metal. My parents and friends seem to understand that grief takes away the appetite, and they don't push back too hard. Perhaps because it's the lesser of two evils: not eating vs. not wanting to live.

I never thought I would be suicidal, primarily because my grandfather committed suicide and I saw how it impacted my parents. I thought I'd never be able to understand the logic of taking one's own life; it's so selfish. He put his family through years of grief and guilt, always wondering if they could have done or said something different.

However, considering J is dead and I'm throwing his clothes on the floor just so I can pretend to do his laundry, it suddenly makes sense. I've already reached the climax of my life, and now the man I was going to have kids with and retire with is gone. I'll never have a family again, because I can't love another man. I married the love of my life and I will be loyal to him forever. So what does that mean the rest of my days will look like?

Go to work, not care about it because my husband is dead, scream at my co-workers inside my head when they talk badly about their husbands, feel my blood boil whenever I see a reckless driver who doesn't realize how close they are to taking away someone's life, punish myself for calling J during lunch (because being on the road one minute earlier could've saved his life), figure out how to answer the question "How are you?" without melting down, endure multiple panic attacks, answer the phone and feign interest in other people's lives, and then ingest Xanax at night so that the nightmares and bloody imagery forcibly stop and I fall into unconsciousness so that I can be rested to repeat the cycle of hell tomorrow.

This isn't a day that I can continue living. I am not living – I am existing. Thus, upon realization of this truth, I start to pace around my house and think of methods for how to end my life. I'm not helping anyone with my life, only adding sorrow, and I can't see a way that anything will ever improve. Suicide seems like a sad but ultimately pragmatic option. Plus, when I die, I'll either be able to see J again, I'll be reincarnated and start a new life without the memories of this one, or I'll just turn to dust. Any of those sounds far superior to the cycle of hell that I'm living in now.

After finally breaking down to my mom when she visits, she signs me up for a widow's group at a local hospital, and I hear the following "helpful" information:

> "The second year is so much worse than the first. At least during the first, you have some shock to protect you. The second year is when the reality finally sinks in."

> "At least I have my kids: They're the only reason I get out of bed in the morning."

> "Even though s/he's gone, I feel so grateful for the time we had together."

> "Holidays suck. Have a timetable, escape routes, and ideas of what you can say to people. It's a good idea to make your spouse's favorite dish, light a candle on the

table, or have an empty chair for them at the table in remembrance."

"God never gives us more than we can handle. We just can't understand His plan."

"I'm actually relieved that the illness is finally over; it was so sad to watch the suffering."

I think after attending these types of sessions, my depression is far worse. I can't quite imagine how much lower I can go in my second year, I have no kids to get me out of bed to feel like my life still has purpose, and I must be the worst wife because I don't feel grateful. I feel so damn angry. And alone. No one else lost their spouse suddenly; they all witnessed a slow decline of life and had conversations about moving forward before death overtook their loved one. They are angry at an illness, while I'm angry at a 100% preventable choice of the woman who killed J while driving recklessly.

So, back to the pacing. The enduring wrench in my stomach and roller coaster with unseatbelted emotions. The desire to end it. The refusal to believe that life can possibly yield pleasant conditions again.

The next time I go to the doctor, he prescribes anti-depressants. He says that my "cup" is not full and that it's okay to need pharmaceutical help. When I go home and take the pills, I just feel numb and lethargic. Alcohol starts to enter my mind, and I drink. And I drink again.

NOW

I'm extremely thankful that my experiment with drinking was short-lived. After a couple weeks of getting drunk every evening, I realized that I hate feeling nauseous and sick. The altered state of mind wasn't worth the consequences. Knowing what I do now about the power of addiction, I'm really thankful I stopped drinking after those two weeks and poured the rest down the drain before it got out of control. I don't want to hurt my family or die an incredibly painful death with liver disease.

Not hurting my family became the light I held onto throughout my depression and grief. Perhaps the most beneficial part of those widow groups was finally meeting a widow whose husband committed suicide. The guilt, shame, and loss she felt was something I knew I didn't want my family to feel or remember when they thought of me. I remember hearing her speak about all the questions that plagued her mind, such as "What if I had done _____?" and "How could he do this to me? Didn't he love me? Was life with me that terrible?"

Even today, when I have my most troubling days – which are remarkably infrequent – I go back to the knowledge above and remind myself that I can, in fact, live for someone else. Six years ago, "someone else" was my friend who needed a listener, my mom who needed her daughter, and my nieces who needed to know they weren't going to lose me too. Today, "someone else" includes my second husband. I never thought I would find another man I could love, or even one who would want to dwell in the brokenness of my life. When we first met (three and a half years after J's death), I talked about my late husband and my hard days a lot. I was sure that I was going to scare him away, for what twenty-something male wants to deal with that?

Sean saw me not as a broken woman, but a woman who had lived life and understood the hardships that tested people to their core. Who found their core. He saw a real person who didn't pretend that everything was perfect, but rather was real and cared about real issues – not makeup, or waist-size, or shopping. He saw the strength and capacity of my heart, because of how deeply I loved. And he knew, so he tells me, that I was a woman who would live with my priorities in the right places.

I became a deep thinker because of those emotions, reflecting on philosophical questions such as: How does one really know great love? Is anything worthwhile in life easy? What does honoring a dead person look like? How have other depressed people in this world found a healthy way through it? Asking these questions became paramount to understanding who I am and how important it is for me to not dishonor J by giving up.

I also received help starting at month 13. My outside help consisted of two trauma therapists who kept my exploration of putting-one-foot-in-front-of-the-other on track. This consisted of talk therapy, meditative practices, and eye movement desensitization and reprocessing (EMDR) to reduce panic attacks. Perhaps the most important lesson I learned through these women was that while the pain will never go away completely, I can control its size. I was skeptical about the word "control" for a long time, because all my reactions felt so automatic. I was even diagnosed with Post-Traumatic Stress Disorder (PTSD) to account for all my triggers. However, as I kept practicing the coping mechanisms, I learned that water (representing my pain) would not always be boiling; the goal was to make it simmer.

When I felt myself, or still feel myself, building a reaction that I know is leading down a spiral staircase into despair, I can do the following until I find something that helps:

- Smell a strong scent, like cinnamon or lavender, to relax my mind
- Go for a walk and name beautiful things in nature
- Clean something to feel immediate success
- Call a friend who will just listen

14

- Read a children's book, which stirs in me a pleasing recollection of simpler times and reminds me of my real journey (remaining open)
- Rock in a rocking chair
- Stroke my pet's hair and feel his calmness
- Start a new home improvement project, as my relationship with my house is a caretaking relationship and it feels good to nurture something
- Watch my favorite *Star Trek: The Next Generation* episode that so intentionally discusses grief, the human condition of being mortal, and accepting the deaths of people we love (especially Season 3: "The Bonding")
- Make a card for someone I love to tell them their life means something to me
- Boil water for a cup of tea

This list was actually started by the woman who became my best friend: Jessica. We went to high school together but weren't close until she showed up at my house two months after J died to give me a hug. By listening and validating my intense emotions, she helped me create pockets of time that weren't overflowing with pain; she taught me that verbalizing could diffuse my strong reactions. I even saw that as she talked about the hardships in her life, it was nice to switch roles and listen to her. I guess it was the beginning of feeling purposeful. It grew as my friend invited me to her special education classroom to have lunch with fifth graders who desperately needed a mentor/consistent adult in their lives. This happened after 20 months. I was so anxious about meeting these girls, wondering how could a depressed person be a positive role model? Well, it somehow happened by seeing their pain and how much they looked forward to our lunches. No hugs in my life compared to those when they saw me walking down the hall. Becoming a source of happiness to fifth graders in North Minneapolis proved to be quite a healing mechanism, as it made me start to feel alive again.

If I had to be alive, it was becoming clear that my life could help someone else. There are so many people who are hurting. Accordingly, I became a teacher and now meet regularly with students navigating grief and depression. I listen, encourage them to be honest, share vulnerabilities and art that helped me cope, and promise to be there when they need me. The hope I give others is definitely something worth living for, and it drove me out of depression.

One final note about depression: Yes, it is a diagnosable illness, and some people do need drugs. But many well-respected scientists believe drugs are only one way to treat it. Exercise and gratitude meditation are highlighted every year as being more helpful than most prescriptions. Check out the Center for Investigating

Healthy Minds through the University of Wisconsin-Madison where they evaluate brain patterns in different types of people to assess changing the depressed brain. Drugs don't have to be *the* answer.

Chapter 3: Being "Strong"

"J would not want you to cry and give up. Make him proud of you! Be the strong woman he loved. Everyone has pain."

Does strong mean that I bottle up all my feelings and try to live every day with a smile on my face? Being fake? Who are you to decide what correct grieving or living looks like? You tell me to be grateful and live fully because I have to live for him now, too. Of course I was lucky to have J as long as I did, but I can't be grateful right now. I am so angry that this happened to me, to him, to our life! Maybe my honesty about my ingratitude sounds selfish, but I was robbed. You get to go home to your life and take it for granted.

Almost every musician has songs about love and the feeling of what-would-I-do-without-you, right? In high school or college, we read the suicide of Romeo and commented on the power of his relationship with Juliet. He couldn't bear to live without her. Ah, true love. Yet if I have similar thoughts and attitudes, I'm told that I'm prolonging my misery. If I want to talk with J and figure out a way to still live as his wife – believing that he is still here and I just cannot see him anymore – I am looked at as crazy and clingy. At John F. Kennedy's funeral, his brother Robert read this excerpt from a 1910 sermon by Henry Scott Holland, and it was not looked at as crazy:

Death is nothing at all.
I have only slipped away to the next room.
I am I and you are you.
Whatever we were to each other,
That, we still are.
...
Life means all that it ever meant.
It is the same that it ever was.
There is absolute unbroken continuity.
Why should I be out of mind
because I am out of sight?
...

I am but waiting for you.
For an interval.
Somewhere. Very near.
Just around the corner.
All is well.

     I don't want another life, and I don't want to feel better. Those are steps away from J. I feel like several people imply that I dishonored him by resigning from a prestigious job three months after he died to stay home for a while. They think that staying busy with work is the answer, but what experience do they have that's relevant? I can only push my conscious nightmares about the crash and desire to die so far down within my soul before it explodes into hyperventilation or is blown away into apathy.

     Finally, "everyone has pain," huh? That may be true, but pain affects people differently and in heightened quantities. It's not the same. Most people experience expected deaths (i.e., parents, aunts, uncles, etc.) and hear of a tragic young person's death. They truly feel more than low for several months and experience a wave of regrets that they wish could be changed. Perhaps they even tell themselves: "I'm not going to take anything for granted again. I'm going to make time to call my friends and keep in touch with older relatives. I'm going to search for a job I truly enjoy."

While people in traumatic situations can appreciate knowing that others are trying to be better people, it would be nice to receive an acknowledgement that they cannot grasp the whirl of sudden death. They don't know what it's like to pace every night in your house because you can't get terrifying images of tire marks over your husband's body out of your mind. They don't know what it's like to fantasize about grabbing a hammer and smashing the autopsy report that sears the synapses of your brain. They don't know what it's like to want to remember the good times, and then spiral down into darkness because those times are gone at the hands of a reckless driver. They don't know what it's like to wonder, every day, who is going to die next? If your brother is 10 minutes late, should you call him? If he doesn't answer, should you start dialing hospitals? They haven't been told that you have to change your house, because if you leave it as is, it will become a museum that you eventually resent.

NOW

After reading powerful biographies, especially Elie Wiesel's Holocaust narrative *Night*, I know that strength has nothing to do with being silent, or creating some brave front. I don't bring up Wiesel because I think there is a comparison between the tragedy of the Holocaust and my personal situation; mine is far easier. However, I did learn a lot from that book about the commonalities of survival.

For example, when I force myself to answer the question: "Why didn't Wiesel give up?", I find that he does subtly tell me. On the 42-mile death march, he doesn't give up because his father is running beside him and needs his physical presence to keep going. I know today that I cannot give up because there are people who need me and find value in my life. As a teacher, I end up sharing my story with many young people who have gone through or are presently experiencing deep loss – and this brings possibility.

Before my students, I knew I could not give up because of the suffering it would cause my parents. I tell my students that, too, and many of them open floodgates about dealing with suicidal thoughts; they need to hear that adults have them, too, and find a way to persevere. Regardless, I have learned that I need to not only be here on this earth, but also to be present because my life matters to someone. At every night of parent-teacher conferences, at least a handful of parents will tell me how their teenager loves my class, despite the tough grading, because I give them courage to open up as an individual.

Other commonalities from Wiesel's narrative are believing in something (not necessarily faith), finding people who are in the same situation to walk with you, and acknowledging that the future is not doomed to be exactly like today. An aphorism that I enlarge for my classroom wall is "The only certainty in life is that nothing is certain; things change." Sometimes this brings great distress, because we are comfortable with what life is like now. I am comfortable writing my thoughts to you, reflecting on how far I've come in the journey of grief. However, I know that my life is not exempt from future traumas and deaths, and when they happen, I will probably be angry at the world all over again. BUT, I do know that the next time my life is on the major roller coaster and I'm barely hanging on, I will have past experience and wise people to help me shape my response. Will that make it any easier? Possibly, but that's not the point. The point is that I'm not going to worry about finding a way to stay alive and cope – I know that I will find a way. Furthermore, that experience will allow me to connect with others who are hurting, and if that's not the purpose of life, I'm not sure what is.

There are widows who push everything down, get pregnant in six months, and force a new life without taking the necessary time to honor the past. There are widows who throw themselves only into work, or drugs, or taking care of their children. I've met these people, and they would agree that they feel anything but strong. Strength is being able to face your fears and death, talk about the spouse you loved, and utter the words "I'm not okay." It's okay NOT to be okay. It's called being real/honest/human/in love/in loss.

Chapter 4: Expressing Anger

THEN

I f***ing hate the world. God. Reckless drivers. My job. My house. My empty house. Being a widow. Explaining what happened. Motorcycles. People who take their spouses for granted. Unfairness. Loneliness. Trite platitudes by people who've never been severely touched by death. The phrase "moving on." Being young. Comparisons with other widows. Not dying with him. Guilt that I could've done something. The need to get out of bed. Planning a funeral. Doing paperwork for insurance. Opening the mail. Responding to the mail. Going grocery shopping for one. Thinking about my "old" life dreams. Changing verb tenses: J likes – liked – helping me make dinner.

I also hate feeling the emotion of hate. Because I am boiling with rage internally, my veins are about to pop out of my head like someone is coiling their fingers around my neck and squeezing. I want to scream at the top of my lungs, but when I try, odd sounds come out because I'm also gasping for air and attempting to keep my eyes' floodgates closed. When I'm really physically worked up, I'm scared because I feel so out of control. Taking deep breaths sounds like the dumbest solution in the world; it's too simple.

What's more is that society isn't comfortable hearing about death. Especially from a young widow or mother because the age reminds them that senseless deaths can happen to them or their kids, too. Thus, if I try to express my anger, most people will not validate, listen, or get mad with me; instead, they force me to calm down. This doesn't work – it just suppresses and then compounds the anger. And it makes me feel even more alienated because it's the only thing that feels real.

NOW

After six years, I see anger as being a critical first step. I no longer boil with rage, but it does simmer within me from time to time. I thoroughly believe that I needed to let my rage explode – over and over and over again – in order to prevent suppression and naturally find a point of sadness.

Of course I was sad from the beginning, but it wasn't the same. When all my anger was finally let out (three years later), I reached a point of pure sadness that allowed me to make decisions about my future. (FYI, our society may be even more uncomfortable with deep sadness than with deep anger.)

For example, I used to keep all the possible pictures of J in my house displayed. For almost a year, I tried to interact with his spirit like we could still live as husband and wife. My therapist pointed out to me that I was creating a museum, and that this would lead to jailing myself inside. With time in "jail," I would eventually resent J for entering my life, for dying, for preventing me from living the rest of my years. Obviously, this is the last thing a widow wants to feel for her spouse. My point in telling you this story is that when I felt anger, I wanted to scream at my therapist for this suggestion because she was pushing him away. When my anger passed, I understood my therapist's concern that I was creating unhealthy habits that would prevent me from moving forward (not moving on – that's different and unhelpful). I began to comprehend that one cannot live in memories and cherish them at the same time.

However, wise statements like "Memories are meant to be cherished, not lived in" do not always help. Sometimes you have to distract yourself with activities. In fact, I still utilize the activities I found six years ago today because they became a type of focused concentration that re-centered me – like meditation. First, I started learning how to create mosaics because the process begins with breaking things.

Step 1: Go to a garage sale and buy someone's old dishes for $5.00. Alternatively, log onto eBay.com and purchase bags of beautifully colored and cut tile pieces.

Step 2: In an enclosed area outside or in your garage, smash the plates into pieces, saying out loud the unfair or sad reality that confronts you today.

Step 3: Gather the pieces, arranging and then gluing them on a thin wood frame to make a pattern. If you need to trim the pieces to fit, use a tile cutter from a place like Home Depot.

Step 4: Mix dry grout with water, forming mud. Slather it over all the glued tiles, ensuring it fills in all the cracks between the tiles.

Step 5: Wipe the tiles with a warm washcloth so that the grout does not dry on top of them. When the grout is dry, your project is done.

Here is one of my favorite pieces, which hangs in

the guest room of my home:

I also made mosaic picture frames, bowling balls (for a garden accessory), and small tables.

Then I learned another craft: making Ukrainian eggs. This related to my heritage, and I was lucky enough to get a lesson in wax application with a *kistka* (specialized pen) from the largest exporters in the world: the Perchyshyn family who run The Ukrainian Gift Shop in Minneapolis, Minnesota.

Step 1: Using a small, non-electric drill, make a hole in the bottom of a clean chicken egg and drain the yoke.

Step 2: In pencil, section the egg with various symmetrical lines. Draw the pattern that you wish to eventually make permanent.

Step 3: Melt wax inside a *kistka* pen, and then use the tip of the *kistka* to trace over the lines you wish to remain white. The *kistka* will slowly pour out hot wax.

Step 4: Submerge the egg into a jar of colored dye, preferably yellow or gold.

Step 5: Use the *kistka* to place wax over the lines you wish to remain yellow or gold.

Step 6: Gently place the egg into another jar of colored dye, this time a slightly darker color.

Repeat steps 5 and 6 until you submerge the egg into the final background color.

Step 7: Hold the egg over a lit candle, wiping off the melting wax with a paper towel.

Step 8: Cover the eggs with polyurethane and allow them to dry on a drying rack (wood board with nails for holders).

Here is a picture of my Ukrainian egg basket:

I fell in love with making intricate crafts because

they serve important purposes: They distract me for hours, require precision, and enable me to pour out my emotions into something that I can then give away as a gift. That gift indicates a transformation of anger or sadness into beauty every time.

NOTE: As a kid, I was an artist who could barely draw a stick figure. I never thought I'd be able to do anything like this. Maybe one's best work comes out in the midst of intense emotions.

Chapter 5: Logical Guilt

THEN

When your spouse dies suddenly, there are many seemingly logical conclusions to draw about the minor things you could have done to prevent the death. The most common is a telephone call, and this was no different in my case. J left home after lunch to go to work when we ended our phone conversation; if I had just told him I loved him a few more times, that extra 30 seconds would've placed him in front of a different driver – not the negligent one who killed him.

Similarly, it was my decision to teach him how to ride a motorcycle, and if he had been in a car, airbags and a metal frame may have saved his life. Yes, he wanted to learn how to ride himself, but only because his wife loved it. J grew up with a brother and father who rode motorcycles and was not tempted to ride until he married me. Thus, I am the only person to blame for his interest in riding a death machine. Why didn't I do more research about the percentage of riders who die each year? If I had, there's no way I would have become a rider, right? But then I remember thinking, "We'll stop riding once we have kids." That statement certainly depicts that I knew its danger.

What a spouse I was. While I wasn't the negligent driver who rear-ended and dragged him on the road, I placed him on equipment that pretty much guarantees death around a bad driver. We don't live in a world where if you're a good driver, everything will be okay. I should have known, I should have anticipated, I should have been more confident in myself. The only reason I learned how to ride a motorcycle in the first place when I was 19 years old was to prove that I could take a risk and be an interesting person. And four years later, the love of my life paid the ultimate price for my insecurity.

Easy to follow, right? That's the danger of logical guilt. No matter how many times people tell me that I can't blame myself, it always sounds to me like "The only way you are going to move forward is if you let go of these unhelpful feelings." That's not truth; it's self-manipulation.

NOW

As much as I would like to tell you that all those feelings of guilt have gone away, the truth is that they haven't. It is certainly plausible that had he traveled in a car on August 14, he'd still be alive. <u>However</u>, I have accepted that the accident was not close to being my fault. Furthermore, I have accepted that guilt is a very poisonous emotion, which covers two deeper emotions: anger and fear. I was angry that he died, that a reckless driver killed him, that reckless drivers get to live, and that society viewed J poorly because many motorcyclists don't care about safety. I was afraid that other people I loved would die at the hands of reckless drivers too, as there seem to be so many. What if they died doing an errand for me or coming to visit me? How could I live with the knowledge that they'd be alive if only I had run my own errand?

Eventually, I unpacked these questions with people I trusted. One time we played out the scenario that my parents died en route to visit me. This was incredibly scary, and that was the point. They helped me brainstorm everything I would need to do and people who would help me with their affairs. This morbid activity aided my mind by dealing head-on with fear. Most importantly, they scolded me for being so controlling: Did I really believe that my parents would stay away from their daughter because I was scared they would die? Did I really believe they would drive in dangerous weather conditions? They have free will to make their own choices.

This discussion of free will eventually broadened to include J and the woman who killed him. They both had free will, too. J drove that motorcycle because he loved it, and he was the pinnacle of safety in a reflective vest, a white helmet, and all leather. But no matter how safe someone is, they aren't protected from the consequences of another's actions. The woman who killed him made choices to drive dangerously: on her phone, speeding, without insurance. Her choices yielded the ultimate consequence.

Yes, he still would've had a chance of survival if it hadn't been for me teaching him how to ride that motorcycle. Logically, his survival would've been higher had he never met me. But the universe brought us together because we were meant to be together. J wasn't supposed to die – I don't believe that God scripts every part of our lives. If He did, how on earth could we have free will? How would there be unintended consequences?

J's father and sisters tell me frequently – probably every time we speak – that J was never happier than when we were married. That I completed him. And he told me similar sentiments many times throughout our marriage. He loved me for me, and that included the insecurities that were a part of my story and shaped who I was. **If I could somehow go back in time and erase the motorcycle from**

my history, what else would change in my timeline, in my priorities, in my activities? Would I still meet him?

The purpose of asking these questions is that they cannot be answered. We cannot know how our lives would be different if we remove one of the threads within our life's tapestry.

J's favorite *Star Trek: The Next Generation* episode of all time (we were both serious geeks) was called "Tapestry" for this very fitting line: "There are many parts of my youth that I'm not proud of. There were... loose threads – untidy parts of me that I would like to remove. But when I... pulled on one of those threads – it unraveled the tapestry of my life." In this episode, the Captain is dying as a result of a problem with his artificial heart. An omnipotent alien offers him a new heart if he goes back in time and prevents the fight that ended with a sword in his chest (thus creating the need for the artificial heart). He has to change the arrogant, undisciplined man of his youth. The Captain does make the changes and is transported back to his present – but it's not the one he remembers. Instead of being a captain, he's a low-ranking science officer who never took a risk in his career. His life turned out completely different.

Many of us spend time thinking, "Oh, if only I had handled that situation differently, my life would be so much better." But Captain Picard's reflections exemplify an important truth of the human condition: Our loose threads/untidy parts/messiness sculpt our lives. There is no point or helpfulness in trying to change it. All we have is the present moment to love and enjoy. Of course I wish J were here to enjoy it with me. But I have his legacy, his story, and his love that are a part of me now and influence other people as I speak about us and try to honor him. It is all I can do, and it lets me live knowing that he is smiling down on me.

Chapter 6: Physical Touch and Loyalty

THEN

My mom notices my poor posture as well as my lack of sleep. She deduces that a massage will help me relax. However, when she brings it up, I recoil. Massage was a very special nightly gift that J gave to help me fall asleep, and I do not want anyone else's hands on me now. It will feel wrong, like a replacement of him.

Being so close to another person that you touch is a very intimate act. Perhaps it was just the way I was brought up, but I was even initially uncomfortable when my best friend put her arm around me and stroked my hair on the couch. While I knew that her intentions were to lessen my feelings of isolation, anything more than a quick hug felt strange and somehow disloyal to J. He was where I sought comfort, intimacy, and protection. No one else can just sweep in and fill his roles. If I let them, then it must mean that I didn't love him as much as I thought I did.

After all, a widow stands alone. A loyal widow has no substitutes – no one to talk to like her husband, no one to cook for like her husband, no one to laugh at all their jokes, no one to make a holiday enjoyable. These simple things are beautiful parts of marriage, and sharing them with others seems to be just another part of the disintegration of that life that I loved.

NOW

The turning point for accepting touch again actually came two years after the accident, with a weighted blanket in my therapist's office. One day, when my thoughts were in a paper jam and I was having great difficulty staying in the present to work through my emotions, my therapist told me to grab the heavy blanket to my left and cover my body. Both sides were made from micro-fleece and stuffed with small pellets; the weight totaled 16 pounds. Within minutes of fixing the blanket to cover my legs, arms, and shoulders, I felt calmer. I didn't want to move – there was something about this heavy blanket that made me feel secure and my emotions confined/less all-over-the-place. I asked my therapist why this blanket seemed to make me feel better. What was the logic?

She said that weighted blankets have often been used for people in trauma. She said that "normal" people can't stand the feeling, because it's so constricting. But people who've been through trauma feel safer and their thoughts less intense under the blanket. As I researched, I found that many people use them to sleep, and many parents use them to control their children's tantrums. The consensus is that the physical confinement yields mental calmness as well.

Using the blanket also made me realize how much I missed the physical pressure from someone's touch. If I used touch to relieve pain and PTSD symptoms, that would make J happy. For the first couple of years, when people would look at how I was living my life and ask, "What would J want you to do?" or "If roles were reversed, what would you want for him?", I dismissed their questions right away as uninformed and unhelpful. And they were at that time. However, as the years began to stack, I thought about meeting J in the after-life. I no longer saw myself crying, explaining that I just couldn't live without him. Instead, I saw myself telling him how much I missed him, and that I did my best to live life after he died, honoring him with my choices, remembering him fondly, and striving to help others the way he always did.

Once I had this revelation, I knew that I had to reframe how I perceived simple things like massage and complex things like my work.

Prior to the accident, I was a business analyst for a state agency that worked on collaborative technologies for criminal apprehension. Though it may sound dry, I thoroughly enjoyed it. After a month off to deal with paperwork and grief, I decided to go back to work part-time. Proudly, I tried for two months to get back into the swing of my routine. But it didn't work. My emotions controlled me to such an extent that I was ineffective and could not concentrate. I resigned, decided to move across the city, and began intensive grief therapy.

Moving across the Twin Cities from the far east to the far west helped immeasurably with concentration, as I bought a house that needed to be nurtured. In many ways, this was my first art project (see Chapter 4) and my first new relationship. The house needed everything from internal plumbing repairs to new lights and floors. I took classes at Home Depot in order to tile my upstairs bathroom with slate and my kitchen backsplash with ceramics. I felt renewed pride and excitement in my work as the house began to look modern and showcase bold colors. The best parts were that I could do it alone and tell my stories to the walls. It was a new place that didn't have intrinsic memories of J, though it was certainly a healing place where J was discussed. My house allowed me to feel a sense of productivity when I had energy and pass time until I discovered the next chapter I could enter.

When enough time passed, I knew that to honor J, I needed to find something meaningful to do with my life. Especially something that would allow me to talk about him, coping mechanisms, and how to deal with loss. Pretty perfectly, I found a new career teaching high school English, as I've mentioned before. It could not be better suited for me as my classes discuss philosophical problems and themes surrounding the human condition, as well as write about people and experiences that define them. I am privileged to have found that job and those many students; we've greatly influenced each other's lives.

I hug those kids. They hug me. And once a month after work, I get a professional massage before I come home and find my next home improvement project. The massage is relaxing, and it soothes my back pain. The projects are challenging and affirming.

Chapter 7: Other Widows

THEN

It seems like there is no one in my particular situation. I've tried four widow gatherings, and they consist of mostly elderly people who lost their spouse to a long battle with cancer. If there happen to be a few middle-aged people in the crowd, and they lost their spouse to a sudden heart attack, all they talk about is how their kids are the reason they keep getting out of bed in the morning. All of these people had a long life with their spouse, and none deal with a death directly caused by a negligent driver. These widows/widowers aren't triggered multiple times a day, reliving the death whenever they see bad drivers on the road, any kind of accident, any motorcycle, etc. They don't have a 16-page gruesome autopsy report, and everyone isn't telling them: "Hey, you're young. You can find someone else."

Even though I know it's wrong to compare one person's pain to another's, I can't help but feel jealous that they got to say goodbye, that they had conversations about death with their spouse, that they have a true support network (whether it's their kids or all the other similar widows). It seems they have it so much easier.

When I finally connect with a 34-year-old widower, it is online through a message board called Chapter Two's Young Widow Bulletin Board. I connect well with him because he lost his wife in a motor vehicle collision the same summer that I lost J. We become friends over the phone, sharing stories for hours about our spouses. He was only married for six months, and due to his military enlistment, only lived in the same city with her for one month. They were very much in love, and it is heartbreaking to hear him more depressed than I. I learn that men are expected to "get over it" much quicker than women, and of course, not show tears. He also tried to find widow groups in his state and found the same types of people I did: very kind, but in a completely different situation.

Due to this loneliness, my new friend turned to his music, and at times, to drugs. Drugs were a vice in his past, and after his wife died, he found no living reason to exist in a clear, sober reality. While I understand his logic, I am very scared for him. One of the things we do in our conversations at night is promise each other that we won't give in and end it (our life). I wish he lived here. I need a friend that doesn't live so far away.

NOW

Time has honestly quelled my once comparative nature. I came to realize that those older widows and widowers suffered through more than I perceived: They had to watch their spouse in immeasurable pain for an extended period; ride the medical roller coaster of changing doctor's opinions and treatment options; help their child(ren) cope with the loss of a parent; and because of their long marriages, rediscover how to exist as individuals. For their adult lives, the pronoun was "we," not "I." Their kids help them get out of bed, but the business of being a now sole parent often means suppressed grief and never letting down the mask that tells the kids: "It's okay." As I pass the six-year anniversary since J died, I see that these older widows are still going to the hospital groups; I haven't been to those in three years. Was their forced suppression of grief to take care of others preventing any kind of healing?

The other wonderful lesson I learned is that people who haven't lost a spouse can still profoundly understand grief and pain. And they can yield important sensitivity by listening and saying things like "I can't imagine how hard this is." My best friend, Jessica, would listen to my heartache and fears and try to help me problem-solve through the lens of being my friend, knowing that grief takes a lot of time and energy from people. While she has not lost any immediate connections in her life, she's observed them again and again as a special education teacher for students in extreme need and trauma. She's also felt a great deal of personal loss in her life, through relationships ending in betrayal and violence in her home. No one connected more with me, and we had very similar feelings as we processed our lives over the years, despite having such different circumstances.

In the last couple of years, something strange has also happened with other widows I meet. As I no longer have the deep, guttural need to be in support groups in order to make it to the next day, I am able to be much more open and share short, meaningful moments with people. For example, I was looking at buying a new house last year, and when I found out the seller was newly widowed, my heart just sank for her. She ended up coming back to the house as my realtor and I were locking up, and thus we were able to say hello. To this stranger, I simply said the following: "I am so sorry to hear about the loss of your husband. There's nothing worse." She looked into my eyes and understood that there was more to my second line and said, "You know?" I replied, "Yes, my husband was killed in a crash five years ago." No more words needed to be said; she opened her arms and we embraced. These kinds of moments do not happen infrequently.

I often hear about a friend's friend or sister who is a widow and still impacted on the anniversary of their husband's death. In my first two years, I would've said (in my head, of course), they're only impacted on one date now?! But as I approach the six-year mark, I know what they mean. Life has moved forward to the extent that people change and grief is no longer a primary focus. We all still think about our beloveds, but it comes back to a primary focus on the anniversaries. And that's when lots of tears come back and drain our bodies. And you know what? It's okay to lose it then. There's nothing wrong with tears.

Chapter 8: Redefining Success and The Terrible Word "Should"

THEN

Six Months. I can't believe I've become so helpless. I'm so scared of driving that I can't even go to Target without feeling panicked. I hate the sounds of sirens and the sight of motorcycles: They make me relive the image of J being rear-ended and dying on the road. I don't even want to go outside. I used to be such a high-powered individual with a prestigious job and ambitious work ethic. I earned my master's degree at 21 years old – and now I struggle with completing the most mundane tasks for my home or even writing thank you notes. Oh gosh, there are so many thank you notes to write. I should be able to do more than get out of bed and walk to the mailbox today.

Two Years. I just started graduate school to earn my teaching license, which is thankfully only one year because of my previous education. But I often wonder: Can I do this? I have to leave an hour early to avoid rush hour and leave time for breaks when the simple act of driving is too much. I cry when I get there because a half hour of driving feels like trauma. I've even had to leave my night class because some student says the words "car crash" and my mind has a mini-seizure, flooding my thoughts with gory images of my husband. How in the world will I ever be able to be a teacher? Kids will say things, too. I should be able to handle "innocent" conversation! It's been two years. I've been through so much therapy. What's wrong with me that I'm still so triggered and can't sit for 90 minutes until the break?

Four Years. I'm finally able to drive for routine errands and get to my new job on time everyday. It's been a long struggle getting on and off exit ramps and trusting other people when they merge. About a month after I am finally driving without any panic attacks, I get t-boned by yet another woman who isn't paying attention. I was going straight through an intersection, and she turned left right into my door. My whole body is numb. I can't move. They call an ambulance because I can't stop hyperventilating. What kind of sick game is the universe playing with me?

I'm not physically hurt, but in the days, weeks, and months that follow, I'm sliding backwards. Shouldn't I be able to recover more quickly? Shouldn't I be able to maintain some of my progress from all that damn therapy?

Five Years. I'm getting engaged. Should I really be doing this? Can I make it through a second wedding ceremony? Am I just setting myself up to get hurt again? I love Sean and look forward to being with him. Now, what if he dies? What if his patience runs out? What if I can't stop comparing him to J, like the other widows I met? Is this all really worth it? Will I be happy? Like, genuinely happy? I'm still triggered by things people say; I still feel broken at times. I so desperately want to feel normal. I did everything you're supposed to do: therapy, journaling about our life together, volunteering, making time to grieve, connecting with other widows, trying to stay in the present. It still hurts. I still miss him. It's not an everyday kind of ache like it was for the first years, but should I really be getting married if I'm not completely "through/over" this?

NOW

The word "should" is poison. It leads to self-deprecating behavior, more guilt, and unnecessary anguish. It is based in comparison, which doesn't work with the cycle or timeline of grief. Everyone's journey is different.

Many people don't have the extreme fear of driving like I did, but then again, my history before J really fueled that. I was in a pretty horrible car accident three years before I met him, and it led to a year of physical therapy for a permanent injury in my pelvis. I also read and wrote about motor vehicle collisions all the time because my job throughout college was a legal assistant for a personal injury law firm. Hence, having J die from a reckless driver was like freezing rain on a mountain cliff. I learned that I had to acknowledge all these emotions from previous experiences that multiplied when I was sorting through my husband's death. I was so hard on myself for not being normal in the car – I pulled over many times for hyperventilating and couldn't visit my parents who live a few hours away.

In reality, I was being safe. I had a huge mental wound, and it's no less important just because you can't see it. For what it's worth, everyone falls into the "should" world sometimes. It's really hard not to in a society that constantly portrays an image of what our lives should look like. My best friend claims that the fastest way out of the "should" world is acknowledging it and reminding oneself of reality. There are no "shoulds" with the grieving process – other than you shouldn't kill yourself.

Each year following J's death brought its own difficulties. Things that used to be so natural to me, so routine, became so hard. During the first year, I didn't even want to get out of bed; while J and I used to go on hour-long walks, now a five-minute walk outside was the best I could do. But I was trying to take care of myself, and that was a step in the right direction. During the first three years especially, I was petrified of driving, so getting to Target without pulling over for panic attacks became a big deal. And that was okay, too. Those small steps were the blocks to putting my life back together. By the way, it took a long time to accept that these baby steps meant resilience; I often got sucked into the world of "Everybody can do these things except me." I healed more quickly, though, when I acknowledged little successes rather than beat myself up for how small they were. I also realized that I needed to be intentional about surrounding myself with people who were supportive of small successes. There were some times my parents were great, and some times I had to pull away because they weren't helpful.

I also had to re-frame big projects so I wouldn't feel as overwhelmed. I seemed to get stressed out much more quickly than before J's death. Breaking tasks into smaller chunks and labeling what really matters became important steps for getting jobs done and choosing which jobs to do. For example, let's talk about thank you notes. Even though you and I do feel genuinely appreciative that people care and try in their own small way to help, the idea of writing a note anytime someone sends a card or brings over a meal feels hard and inconsequential. *Thanks for bringing over lasagna because my husband was killed.* With time, I realized I didn't have to abide by the same expectations of myself as I did growing up: writing notes within the week. When people truly understand grief, they just want you to make it to the next day. If you really have to, break up the cards you feel you need to write into groups of people: family, work colleagues, in-laws, etc. Or give yourself an amount of time to spend on it each day. Writing notes of appreciation, especially when you feel so angry at the world, can be one of the hardest things to do.

Finally, I was worried about being ready to re-marry up until the hour I took my vows. But I now believe, after meeting more and more people in trying situations, that we are rarely ready for anything. What matters is having enough time and facts to make an informed decision. It will always still be a risk.

Chapter 9: Loving Again

THEN

No one can ever take my husband's place. I would never want anyone to do so. I found my one soul mate on this earth, and now he's dead. This means the wife and mother-to-be in me is also dead. I guess I will be that widow who becomes a great aunt, gives her time to her career, and takes care of her aging parents. I can still have a full and purposeful life.

Yes, I know I will be lonely. Yes, I know I'm young and that many widows eventually choose to remarry.

But what about the many widows who do remarry, only to get divorced a few years later? I met three of them within the first six months after J died. Each told me the same story: After years of grief, they met a kind man. The man listened to their heart and made them feel safe and less alone. They thought, "Maybe it's time I try to move forward and have a different retirement than I previously planned." Slowly, they took down the pictures of their late husband, sold their house, got remarried, and did their best to call another man "husband."

Within a year, problems emerged. The new husband was no longer as patient when hearing about his wife's prior experiences and history, and he felt constantly compared. How could the wife not compare her two husbands, even a little? Yes, the men are different people, but they have the same role. A spouse is one's best friend because you share life together, your living space, your sexuality, your family members and friends. How your new spouse reacts and what he does or doesn't do (positive or negative) is of course going to be obvious. Unfortunately, it often translates into disappointment, and a spouse can feel that, even if it's not said.

These women I met are now divorced, and only one initiated it. That woman, Jane, told me that she felt like she was living a lie. Even though she respected and liked her second husband, she found in time that she was only trying hard to love him. When she closed her eyes, she still wished he were her first husband. And he didn't deserve that, so she filed for divorce. She looked me straight in the eyes after this story and told me not to replace J, but to find love elsewhere in my life. We can only truly give our hearts once.

As I continued to reflect on this in the first six months, a memory of J resurfaced. It was the one and only time we talked about him dying, and the context began as a joke. We were talking about his beloved car – a sports car that he dreamed about since childhood. While I honestly thought it was a waste of money, it was an important symbol to J: something no one could take away from him. Growing up in an unstable family that experienced more than a dozen moves and a house fire, that symbol became something I accepted. Besides, it was J's one indulgence; he was exceedingly smart and frugal with the rest of our finances. Anyway, one night we were discussing this car, and he said: "If I died, you'd never sell the Cobra, would you?"

I responded with a "No, I now see that as a family heirloom and will one day pass it down to one of our kids." I remember that I didn't end the conversation there. I brought up my Uncle Mike, who had lost his wife, my favorite aunt, to a brain tumor in 2001. Less than two years after her death, Mike remarried. At their wedding, I was in tears because I saw my aunt replaced so suddenly; however, my wise father told me to have a different perspective: Mike loved being married so much that he's now honoring my aunt by continuing with his life and committing to marriage again. Ever since I heard those words, they've stuck with me. So I asked J, "Would you remarry if I died?" He looked absolutely shocked and told me that he would never love another.

Thus, once he died, that statement felt like the last nail in the coffin. I would never love another either.

NOW

At the time that I'm writing this chapter, I've in fact been remarried for one year. I started dating after three and a half years passed. And somehow, I'm happy and know it was the right decision.

I still miss my first husband. I still think about him, cry about him, and need to talk about him. I fear that my new husband will die like him, and I will be a young widow twice. Additionally, my new husband has felt compared to J, and we've needed to talk through that more than once. And you know what? It's worth it. The hard conversations, the fear of losing him, the strange feeling of loving two men, the pull of the past and the desire to live in the present. It truly feels like an ever-changing kaleidoscope, where my broken pieces fashion new patterns that I never imagined possible.

At three and a half years, I was having dinner with a group of friends, a couple of them widows in their 40s. Both decided to start a conversation about eHarmony and how much more life there is yet to come. One of them knew about the memory of J saying he would never remarry, and she told me that I have to remember the context at that time: We hadn't been married a year. She said that no one in his or her first year of marriage thinks about remarrying or wanting to be with someone else. Furthermore, I was J's most significant relationship, and he had been lonely for years before he met me. J would not be happy if I spent the rest of my life in relationship isolation. He wanted me to be happy, above all else, and loved the thought of me raising children.

I rebuked my friend's idea at first, claiming that I could not possibly love another man. The response was, "You can always see what's out there without any kind of commitment – maybe you will even find a widower who is more understanding than you can imagine." I have to admit a part of this plan intrigued me. I mean, if I met a widower, maybe his expectations of me "letting go" would be a lot lower. I know, how romantic, right? My friends offered to help me set up a profile online, and a month later I decided to give it a try.

I didn't meet any widowers. But after reading dozens of profiles for two months, I decided to go on dates with two men. The first held rather ordinary/typical conversation at a restaurant and stirred no feelings inside me. The second became the man I just married. Our first date began at a coffee shop in January, then led to a walk by a frozen lake, then on the frozen lake, and ended with climbing trees. Every part of that day had me engaged, as we discussed methods to change the world, real *Star Trek* science, and the losses of our lives. He listened so empathetically as I told him about J. He didn't compare his losses to mine, but they were significant: three friends who committed suicide in college.

As our time together unfolded, I realized that he knew about feeling guilty, hopeless, isolated, and desolate. Even though he wasn't a widower, he made me feel understood by sharing his deep pains and responding to mine with such kindness. This kindness is something I continue to see every week that we're married. He surprises me with his thoughtfulness and genuine desire to understand whatever I'm going through (relating to grief, my job, family, body issues, etc.).

Sean and I dated for one-and-a-half years, and in that time, we went on several trips. Travel is now an important part of our marriage, as it's something I didn't experience with J. I find that the more things unique to my life with Sean, the easier it is to stay living in the present. Despite all my strong beliefs in the first couple years of grief about not being able or desiring to love again, I am so happy that I found a way. I love Sean deeply.

It wasn't an easy road (dating, that is). There were times that I just wanted J, and I usually told Sean to break up with me as a result. But my best friend knew and told me that I didn't really want to break up with him; I was just really scared about him leaving – either by choice or by accidental death. He also saw through my fears and decided the best strategy was reassuring me that I was not broken, that he loved me, and that he loved the person I became as a result of the trauma I've endured. He would tell me that I'm not like most women, and that was a good thing.

I don't know how many people there are like Sean in this world, but I'm willing to bet there are more than lonely people picture in their minds when the dating scene looks so bleak.

Going through a second wedding ceremony was really hard, as I recalled my first vows. However, once I labeled out loud to myself (before the ceremony) that I felt sad about a second wedding, the power of that feeling lifted. This has become an important tool in my coping mechanisms toolkit: Labeling a difficult emotion can diffuse its power. I think it's part of the final stage of grief: acceptance. It doesn't mean we forget, or don't think about our beloveds, but we do come to a point where we understand what death means and have ideas about how we want it to change the rest of our lives. Very few people want to stay in a cocoon, hiding from reality. They want to return to a state of normalcy, but they realize that adapting to a new normal is the only option.

Here is what I have found about Reality:

(1) People need people.

(2) Our hearts can expand to love another person.

(3) Sensitive people will never ask us to replace a loved one.

(4) Loving again does not diminish past love.

Lists like the short one above are yet another coping mechanism of mine. I've found that when I don't know what's true or trustworthy about life/the human condition, it's helpful to make a list of what I know for sure. Some days that list had two items. Some days it held 40.

I leave you with this: I am really glad I found a way through grief, because I am so grateful for life today. I try my best not to take one day for granted, and I don't compromise on anything I believe in. It's been an honor to write this book, and I sincerely hope it is helpful.

Epilogue

Four people in Minnesota died on the icy roads during our first snowstorm of the year last week. When I heard this on our public radio station, I lost it. All my progress was wiped away, and I once again became the fearful widow of years one and two, when the few people in my circle had to text me after they got home, or if they would be more than five minutes late. I required reassurance of safety. During those first years, I was also very cautious about letting anyone new into my life, as they were just an extra worry, an extra death I'd have to deal with.

And now it's been over six years. I've relaxed the five-minute rule to 15 minutes and try to brainstorm other reasons people are late if my brain spirals toward an ugly visualization. I'd love to tell you that all my grief work has eliminated fear's grip, but the truth is I remain haunted that my people – especially my new husband – are going to die. The grip is not as tight as it once was, but when I hear news of a crash, fear coils again around my neck.

Thankfully, that doesn't happen every day. Thankfully, many days when I practice mindfulness, I can acknowledge fear exists without fueling its power. Thankfully, many days I believe my dad's logic that the chance of losing two husbands to car accidents is incredibly minute.

However, if I did lose Sean, there would be something massively different this time around: I would become a sole parent, too. As I am writing this epilogue, I am in my sixth month of pregnancy, and every day my excitement for this new adventure grows. I feel especially blessed because I thought my chance for parenting died with J. As I read dozens of books on parenting and neuroscience in preparation for my little girl, I'm amazed at how much my life has changed in six years. I've even found a name for my baby that symbolizes newness and hope: Ruth.

I first learned about Ruth through a clairvoyant pastor named Beth. She's one of those people that makes you wonder if she's fully human when you look into her eyes, as you feel deep in your gut that you are in the presence of someone holy. I still have much to understand about God and angels, but I think I'm better off not trying to answer every question that arises. What feels right in my heart is the knowledge that there is something greater, and I value the connections that find me when I am open to them. Connections like Ruth.

When I decided to attend a local church for the first time in years, Pastor Beth explained the life of a young widow named Ruth, an alien in a far-away country with only one family member left: her mother-in-law, Naomi. They were incredibly poor and barely surviving. Ruth decided to take Naomi to a new place and look for work; she struggled greatly but was ultimately successful in creating a new life. Not looking, she found a new husband as well, and they became the great-grandparents to King David. There is a lot more to the story, but what stuck with me is this:

Ruth lost everything; her life and plans were broken in many pieces. The only thing to do was take care of the last relationship she still had. But life is often about Plan B, and when we hold up our broken pieces to the Light, they can shift and create new, beautiful patterns. Our lives are kaleidoscopes, and they would not be nearly as beautiful without our complexities and hardships – for those breed our compassion.

At the close of Beth's sermon, she passed around a kaleidoscope, and it now lives in my scariest place: the car. It is by far the most helpful imagery I can assume when I'm in a place of fear. When I think about my little girl, I don't want to shield her; I want to tell her that life is really hard and she will feel broken at times. However, brokenness can lead to newness and patterns that help us as well as other people, sometimes people we don't even know. I want my little girl to go through life with a story of hope to support her in the rough times.

Pastor Beth has helped me see that there are many Christians who don't believe everything happens for a reason. Instead, they believe God puts people in our lives and we are part of an unfolding story in which He walks beside us. I sure wish I'd met her earlier.

At the end of the day, I know that I want to fight against feeling fear because I have such little control over things like the weather, other people's choices, and freak accidents. There is no guarantee of safety for anyone.

However, I also know that fearing Sean's death is normal. It's normal because I'm a wife and he's my husband. It's normal because bad things happen in this world. It's normal because I'm a widow and intimately know how I barely survived. It's normal because I met other widows who had children and, though they all said how their kids gave them something to live for, they often felt trapped, desperate, and unable to grieve as they needed.

So – I may lose it every once in a while, as I did this past week. In those moments, I need to continually remind myself that all my progress is not lost. The truth is that I'm just in a dichotomy of fear: I need to fight the grip and yet accept that it will always be a part of me. This is reality. It doesn't stop me from living or being the person I want to be. It stops me from pretending to be someone I'm not.

Appendix A: Coping Mechanisms Toolkit

(1) Live for someone else when you don't want to live for yourself. It's a way of holding onto hope when you feel anything but positive or worthwhile.

(2) Find your own small coping mechanisms to get through the hardest times: making a cup of tea, meditating on nature, rearranging furniture, talking to the plants, sitting in a rocking chair smelling cinnamon, etc.

(3) Listen to comforting music you know to match your mood, and find new music that doesn't have memories with your spouse attached. Music has such powerful tools to alter a mood.

(4) Get a dog (or a cat). I adopted my yellow lab, Walter, just this year. I can't tell you how good he's been for me. I know that to have a pleasant driving experience to the dog park or to see my parents, I have to be calm for him. And I can somehow do it. He also gets me out for three walks a day and helps me stay in the present by living his life in motion. An animal's presence is a great distraction and comfort. Oh, and pets can't say stupid things.

(5) Use weighted blankets (16-20 pounds). Even though the science was explained to me, I still find it unbelievable how much better I feel after just minutes under a heavy blanket. It truly confines my mind when my emotions feel scattered and scared. Check out vwww.cozycalm.com

(6) Take the time to tell a few select people what's helpful and not helpful. If you're like me and experienced the changing/shrinking address book, investing some time and energy into identifying what makes you explode inside and what feels tolerable from someone else can be really worthwhile (whether it's help cleaning the house, preparing meals, initiating conversations, listening, etc.). I did this exercise with my parents more than a few times, and now we are closer than ever and I can tell them anything – truly. They never judge, never compare me to others in grief, and always make me glad I talked.

(7) Be crafty. Art has some pretty incredible healing properties, which I think stems from the fact that it takes so much concentration. You can't think about your own problems while being artistic, and yet many emotions seem to be released while completing a project. I found mosaics and Ukrainian eggs – what'll be yours?

(8) Help other people. When life sucks, bringing a smile to someone else and knowing that your actions held purpose today can really turn things around. It is the foundation for a meaningful life...even when you don't want one.

(9) Express your grief out loud. Our culture may not want to hear it, but there are people you can find who really do want/need to talk about how much pain they feel. I think even when this is hard because you may compare your

lives, it is ultimately helpful because it validates that grief changes your life. And that it's okay to not be okay.

(10) Choose to spend time with another person, rather than isolate yourself. Be intentional about who will make you feel better with their demeanor – or at least not worse. It's easy to stay under a rock and just say that this life is too much. Everyone I've known has had those moments. But then we hear about people who, 15 years later, still confine themselves to their home and sulk. While this sounds desirable at times, we know it's not what our loved ones want for us...or what will help us feel alive again.

Appendix B: A Few Books That Were Actually Helpful

I Wasn't Ready to Say Goodbye: Surviving, Coping and Healing after the Sudden Death of a Loved One by Pamela D. Blair and Brook Noel (2008, Paperback)

This book is my favorite, written by two women with extreme losses. Their publisher actually distributed the book at no cost to help the families of 9/11 within one week of the tragedy. It contains helpful, different sections for every type of lost relationship (spouse, friend, father, child, etc.). It also includes and debunks grief myths.

Healing after Loss by Martha W. Hickman (1994, Paperback)
I enjoyed this book of daily meditations. It's basically broken up into three sections: (1) interesting quote, (2) reflection of the day, and (3) prayer/meditation/mantra to adopt for the day's particular challenge. Not all of them are at the same high level, but it's the best daily meditation book I found, and I've always recommended it.

The Death of a Husband: Reflections for a Grieving Wife by Helen Reichert Lambin (1998, Paperback)
As a writer, I found solace in the honesty of this poetic collection from a variety of authors. It's also short, so you can read as much or as little as you want.

***Where the Wind Begins* by Paula D'Arcy (1984, Paperback)**

This is a journal of a young woman who lost both her husband and child. She tells stories that make your heart weep, and yet she finds something more by examining the beauty of life.

***Healing Your Traumatized Heart: 100 Practical Ideas After Someone You Love Dies a Sudden, Violent Death* by Alan D. Wolfelt (2002, Paperback)**

This book has the feel of a workbook in that it presents multiple ideas for conversations, projects, and meditations to address the concerns and feelings of life after traumatic death. What I like most is that every page has one thing to do today; it's labeled "Carpe Diem."

About the Author

Michelle Jarvie is an author, educator, and mentor from Minneapolis, Minnesota. She began her career in mediation and business analysis after obtaining a master's in public policy from the Humphrey Institute of Public Affairs. Within two years of graduation, she married and lost her husband, James, to a motor vehicle crash. While searching for hope and coping mechanisms, Michelle quit her job, learned how to remodel a house, and sought trauma and grief counseling for three years.

Sixteen months after her loss, she started volunteering to read with two fifth grade girls who desperately needed a dependable, caring adult in their lives. As a result of this opportunity, Michelle decided to pursue a teaching license in English education. Since graduation in December 2011, she has been teaching creative writing, writers' workshops, and global literature courses at the high school level. She also regularly speaks to large and small groups of teenagers about grief, depression, and moving forward (not "moving on"). She loves to bring in *Star Trek* stories and quotes about grief to supplement her own.

Michelle remarried in June 2013 and, with her new husband Sean, is expecting her first child in February 2015. They love to travel leisurely, stop for great food, and philosophize about changing the world.

Visit her online at http://michellejarvie.com

Made in the USA
Middletown, DE
02 February 2015